song of a lotus leaf

song of a lotus leaf

poems

荷
葉
之
歌

renhui

PRECOCITY PRESS

Copyright © 2020 by Lotus Leaf LLC. All rights reserved

Editor: Brijit Reed
Creative Director: Susan Shankin
Photography: Dawn Li
Additional Image Credits:
> Tobias Durant's photo: "Starry Night Sky"
> Judy Harris' photo: "Magic Food Artist Judy"
> Eamonn Knight's photo: "Good Morning, Good Night"
> James Martin's photo: "Secret Code"
> Lu Tanner's painting: "Rainbow Wind"

Text set in Baskerville

No part of this book may be reproduced or transmitted in any form or by any means, electronic or mechanical, including photocopying, recording, or by an information storage and retrieval system—except by a reviewer who may quote brief passages in a review to be printed in a magazine, newspaper, or on the web—without permission in writing from the publisher.
For permission requests, email the publisher at: susan@precocitypress.com

ISBN: 978-0-9987963-6-9

Library of Congress Control Number: 2020903800

Published by Precocity Press
Venice, CA

First edition. Printed and bound in the United States of America

to the life within me

CONTENTS

PREFACE	XIII
1. SUFFERING	1
i am dawn	2
fateful night	4
i cried	6
rose funeral by water	8
your visit	10
blind cardinal	12
remembering mr. poe	14
transforming pain	16
stress made in america	18
fallen in grace	22
come back to me, heart	24
lotus	26
2. CREATING	29
daily earth wisdom routine	30
connect	32
rainbow wind	34
where is my poem today?	36

	a bouquet of flowers	38
	ocean communion	40
	sing sing sing	42
	flying kites	44
	you went to ames	46
	magic food artist judy	48
	how do we learn?	52
	solace	54
3.	LOVING	**57**
	the heart opens	58
	let me	60
	our paris	62
	good morning, good night	64
	soulmates	66
	closer you come	68
	a night of 100 kisses	70
	mom and dad	72
	our first valentine's	74
	is that you, my love?	76
	waiting, arriving	78
	love promise	80
4.	SEEING	**83**
	petals of the soul	84
	soul song	86
	in spirit	88

lotus effect	90
the invisible S in yin yang	92
one minute	94
i thought i was	96
queen or me?	98
visiting historic staunton	100
laughing santa and buddha	102
starry night sky	104
my last trip	106
5. RETURNING	**109**
the ring	110
secret code	112
circles of harmony	114
full moon night	118
a new day	120
secret symphony at our birth	122
i'm full	124
the ficus tree	126
a river spirit in bliss	128
separation	130
let us celebrate one another	132
into the distance i walk	136
DEDICATION	**138**
AFTERWORD	**140**

PREFACE

"We are born to suffer... and to endure, my dear," said my mother. "Somewhere in your life, you got lost. You felt alienated in a foreign country. You were unhappy in marriage. Made a good living but forgot life. You lost who you really are."

I had wanted to end my life, but the survival instinct woke me up.

I left the self-imposed prisons and hurtful people, and struggled on, traveling the world, seeking healing from the most unlikely places. In the morning, I welcomed the sunrise into my window; at night, I tended my wounds.

I finally learned to laugh and love again, and began to create art and poetry.

"I am touched by every line," my mother smiled at me with tears in her eyes, holding this book, "You are my beautiful lotus leaf rising from a muddy pond."

These poems are witness to a twenty-year transformation— a transplant on my way home.

1. *suffering*

i am dawn

i am dawn
i carry the promise of your day
   when you get up from your bed
and walk upright
   into the shimmering glow
   to work, love, fight and play

i am dawn
i survived a deadly storm
   where seafarers were lost at sea
   and seagulls wailed
   through a darkly night

from the heart of darkness
   i was born

fateful night

that fateful night
i fell from my bed
   to the floor
   as if drawn by
   a web of darkness
i couldn't get up
he was again at his video games
   dead as hell
no mortal in sight
as i was drowning
i saw on my chest
   threads of moonlight—
   the scent of home
i rose

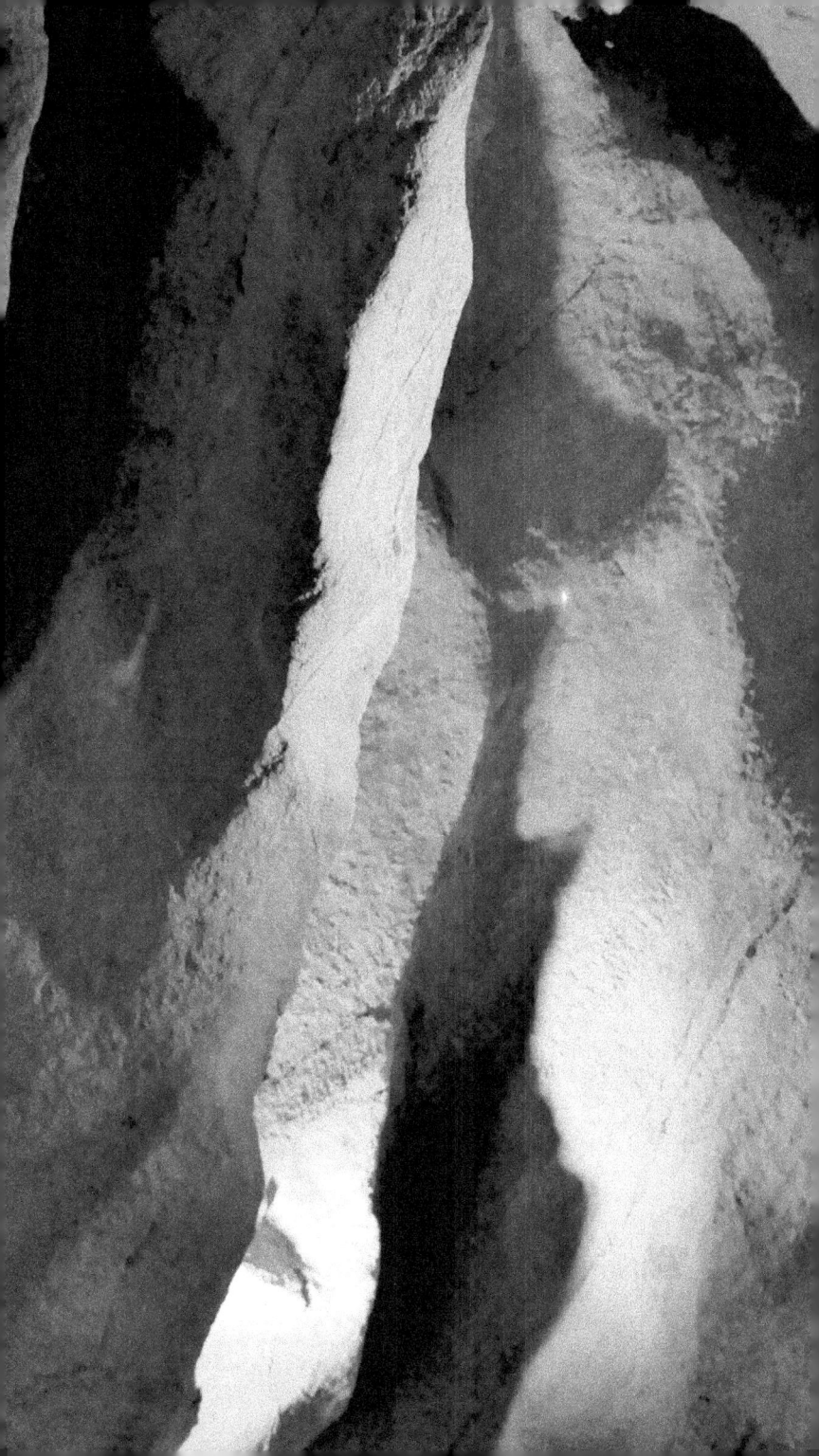

i cried

in the deep
   silent
      velvet
         center of being

i saw you at your garden

you looked at me
   your eyes wet with tears
   your face darkened with sorrow

you opened your mouth to speak
   yet no words came

flowers in the garden moved
and formed the shape of
   a heart

i cried

rose funeral by water

dozens of red roses
   at dusk

petals are torn
   dropped into the river
like blood
   flowing, disappearing

darkness engulfs
   the distant sun

your visit

on a cloudy friday
   when people had gone to work
   and i was sick at home
you came to visit

you entered my humble, half-shaded apartment
   on the outskirts of dc
   with a smile

you brought a bouquet of roses in many colors
   your favorite books, tapes and manuscripts,
   pictures of you and pictures of your parents
   who came from europe and settled
   in pittsburgh in their youth

you stood in the center of my living room
   where i had been for a decade

and opened your memories of your china trip
   the burdened farmers along the yellow river
   your innocent and knowledge-thirsty students
   the passionate peasant woman
   and the misty sacred mountains

you turned into my river
   resonated with the voice of my mother

i cried

it is another friday today
the sun shines through the shaded apartment
   with a smile reminiscent of you
   as ancient as china and as fresh as america

i smile back

blind cardinal

thud
you are at it again
   at my window
taking your reflection
   for your enemy
on a sunny winter day

thud
cardinal at war
your red crest proud like a crown
your beak sharp like a rock

thud
you perch on the tree for a minute
and then go at it again
blindness has become your world

thud
sa sa sa

painful sounds so familiar
   to those inside the window
      fallen to imaginary wars

remembering mr. poe

between the raven and the eagle
   the nevermore and evermore
america chose the latter
   and reserved one day
   for melancholy
   realizing too late that
   depression has leaked
   through all other days
   like mold into the walls

transforming pain

if you are a life form
you will experience pain
how do we transform
   loss to gain?

find a quiet place
look within
revisit the scene of pain
   with tenderness

bring in a power larger than yourself
the sun if it occurred in the day
   the moon if it occurred at night
   your ancestor or mentor who passed you wisdom

let your mind's eye shine on you then
let the light linger
on those who were present—him, her, or them
   and on the surroundings

rivers will wash away our tears
   and splash joy into our hearts

stress made in america

i grew up in china without much to eat
nor decent clothes to wear
or many books to read
yet i was time rich
i was worry free

now that i have a refrigerator packed with food
closets full of clothes
and rooms filled with books
i run out of time every minute
i am restless and anxious

"sweetie, you are still free wednesday night"
"let us go to a concert by the riverside"
"sweetie, out of these hundreds of restaurants
　which ones do you like?"
"don't you have favorites?"

when it comes to choosing a major or a job
it is even harder with more options
there are 5,000 universities and 1,800 majors
i can be in seattle or new york
miami or washington dc
or no, chicago or salt lake city
i can be a doctor or a lawyer
an analyst or an engineer
or no, a meteorologist or an entrepreneur

so many materials to browse—
    ivy leagues and fortune 1,000
many professionals to talk to and internships to work on
hundreds of jobs to investigate and to be interviewed for
and many lines of work in which to wet my feet

barely have i settled on a job
now i must vote for the president
am i a democrat, republican or independent?
how do i know truth from lies in media and journals?
"sweetie, here is another website for you
    to learn about his views"
"sweetie, come to our final fundraising dinner
    for the candidate"
at last i cast my vote for the president

now i must choose a man to be my husband
is it right to choose someone i lusted for?
what if i become pregnant and then get abandoned?
which one of these men would last?
why should i choose a man to love me till the very end?
"sweetie, i found a date for you—
    even though you are on match"
"sweetie, no i do not want to influence you,
    but he is definitely not your type"

should i, would i, could i?
in a paradise of choices and activities
i am pushed into the abyss of excessive stress!
i am a woman making my own living and meaning
not a queen with a kingdom and an army of servants
nor a billionaire with long lines of wise counsel!

fallen in grace

thud!
high heels flew from steep stairs
left arm supporting my body
on march 8 women's day
i fell

911 ambulance
emergency hospital
on call orthopedic doctor did not show
   "your wound is not bleeding outside"
at another emergency hospital,
resident doc hand on chin
   observing in the distance

finally
anesthesia
surgery
five hours of blankness
iv, pain medicine bag
bandaged left arm in a sling
vitals checked every two hours
oxycontin in heavy doses
i became a walking pile of bones
   traversing between the bed to the bathroom

home
in the morning at my window
people going to work or pleasure
   have hastened their steps
i took a walk, a snail walk
   arm in a sling
   palms touching
   as if meditating
i have fallen; i have fallen
   in
   grace

come back to me, heart

in the sacred classroom where knowledge reigns
i read, criticize, reflect, memorize
i've found the language of the mind
but lost the path to the heart

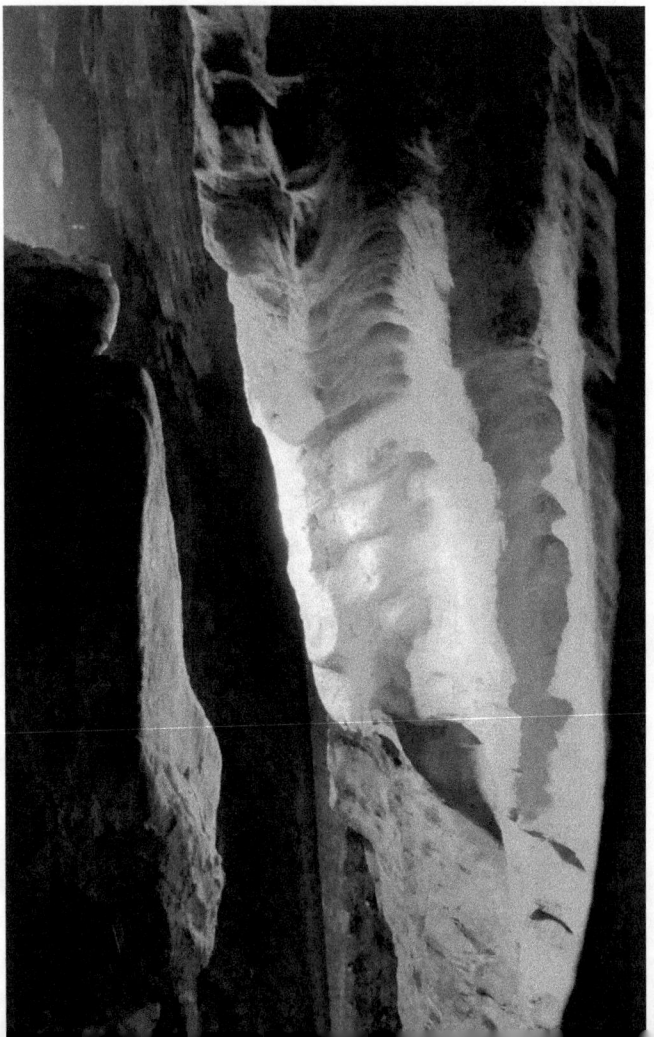

i no longer wander in the forests
fearing violent attacks and intrusions from the back
i no longer fall in love with strangers
fearing fatal wounds and misuses of trust
i no longer open my doors
fearing dust, mosquitoes and burglaries
i no longer go to the church
fearing the confinement of dogmatic preaching

i look at my body in the mirror every day
i cleanse my body with water every day
but i do not know where my heart lies

i grow old, gloomy and cold
i become rigid, stubborn and full of walls

i turn to music, the making of notes
i turn to dance, the initial steps of movement
i turn to singing, the stretch of voice
i turn to paintings, the original lines and colors

i turn to you my love
to the daily embrace of your eyes

oh come to me, heart, the living fresh pounding heart
   the intertwining connecting relating heart
     come back to me
        heart

lotus

bombs

deformed bodies
floating down the mekong river
scarlet sky

in a burning temple
a monk
soaked in gasoline

meditating

lotus

2. *creating*

創

daily earth wisdom routine

stand upright
be rooted like a tree
string an invisible thread
   above your head from the sky
and close your eyes
relax all joints and muscles
quiet your mind
let a column of white light
pour in from the top of your head
   to under your feet
feel the connection
   above and below and all around
feel the suppleness
   within
breathe in the tall pines
breathe in the fresh bamboo grove
breathe in the misty mountain air
one minute
two minutes
fifteen minutes
then tai chi
365 days

connect

after half a century of
sun and moon, wind and water as life
i lost my cool—
my back is bent
my legs give away
my belly is like a woman
   in her last days of pregnancy

i work hard every day
helping people home and abroad
but my body is like a blade of grass
   trembling in the cold

oh, cool, where are you
trees
   sky
   river
   earth
   let me know

"connect
with each step you take
the feet rooted into the ground
   deep like me, the tree
the head aligned to me, the sky
   as if lifted by a thread
the trunk centered and upright
   yet flexible like me, the river
and the whole body relaxed
connected to me, the earth"

each step i take
i connect

rooted aligned relaxed

each breath i take
i connect

rooted aligned relaxed

rainbow wind

you say i am the next van gogh
i am but a humble artist
powered by cosmic rays

i start with a few trees
   a cluster of grass
   or some blurred space

and invite the sun
to twirl in the wind
   at times wildly hot
   at times soothingly cool

they stretch into the open
bursting into
   red flower petals
   white floating lanterns
   black dancing figures
   rotating layers of planets
   or intertwining geometric shapes

rivers bleed through it all in gold
   breaking pain into joy

cosmic curls
in a crescendo of
light, color and passion
   at the still points of my canvas

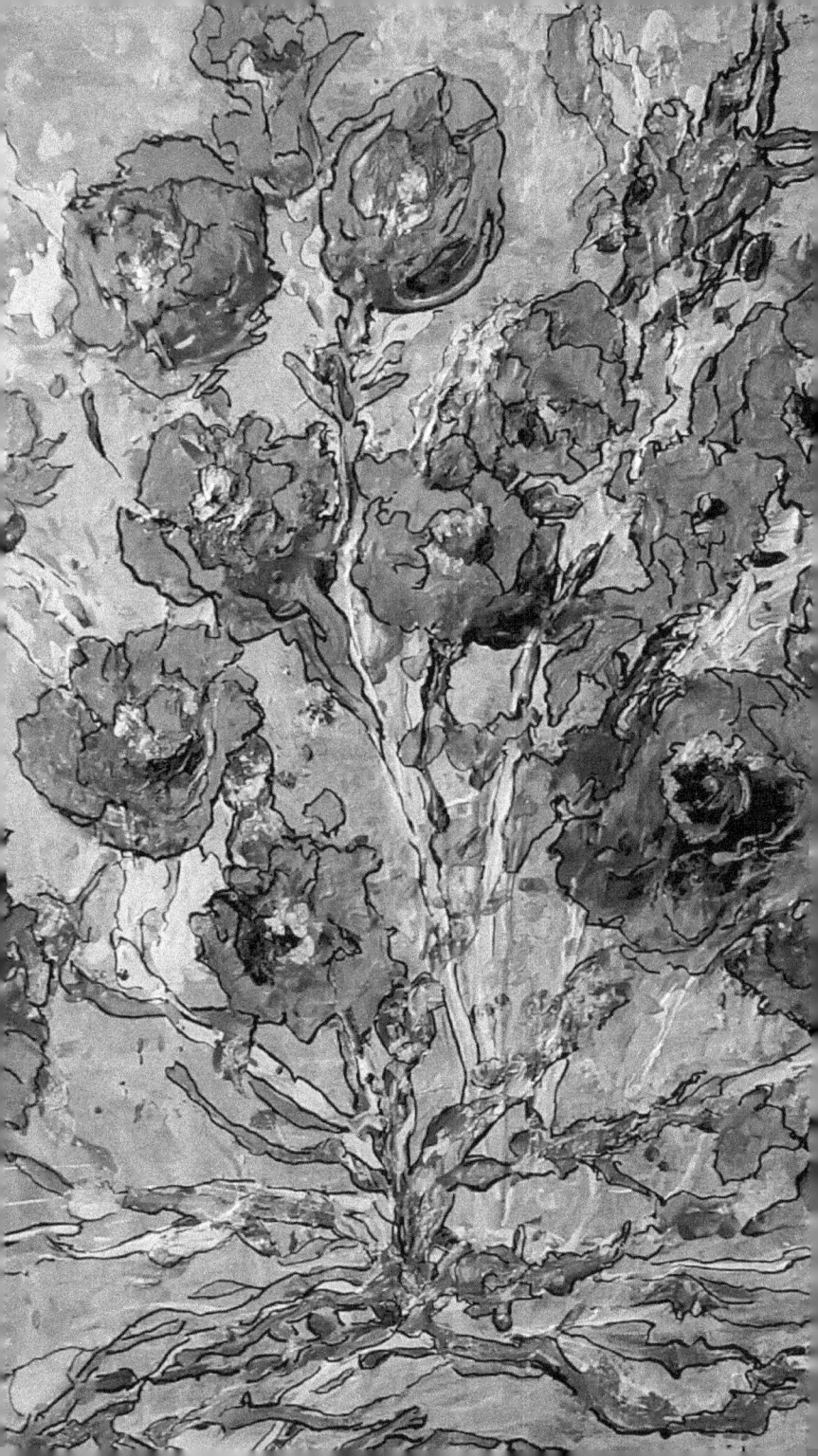

where is my poem today?

"where is my poem today?"
you asked one summer night
   with smiling eyes a little mischievously
"you sent me many lovely poems
   but i did not receive any today"

i was startled
and then laughed
oh, yes, oh!

do you not see the misty moon
in the beautiful sky still slightly blue
above the dancing willows?
that is your poem

do you not hear on this canal road
runners jog, lovers kiss
and birds echo in cheerful tones?
that is your poem

do you not feel
in our walks and talks, songs and dances
that my heart sings when i am with you?
that is your poem

every morning you wake up with the dawn
   inspired
that is your poem

a bouquet of flowers

on a spring night in may
you brought me
a bouquet of flowers from your garden
stems still fresh with dew

oh, what flowers!

the purple and white irises
with their velvet gowns
flowing elegantly as if in a dance

the crimson peonies
with their sunburst beams
so open and generous

and the pink and yellow roses
with their circles of petals
wrapped around in ecstasy!

each flower a piece of heaven
bursting in its own beauty
bearing the original essence of creation

each flower grown and picked by you
a scholar with caring hands
a lifelong gardener

ocean communion

it is so joyful to create
many artists work with brushes and words
you with water, wood and stones

by the eastern shore
on a green peninsula
a vision was born

the foundation
the lighthouses
beams and rooms
a well becomes a pool
piers stretch out into the waves

every evening
when rainbows arch over the horizon
sea spirits gather here with you for the communion
   soaking up the elixir of the ancient souls

sing sing sing

roses, romance, rhymes
hearts, harmony, hearth
all is one—one is all

when you get up from your bed and touch the floor
do you not touch it all?
the roots, the spine, the sky
coming home in every cell?

yes i am all
traveling the world in my home

the all is me, the all is you
the all is love as gentle as the dove

sing sing sing
flowers and bees
the sun and the moon
you and me

sing sing sing
tears and smiles
fears and triumphs

sing of love

born of love
live to love
return
   to love

flying kites

when i was young i loved to fly kites
i was out all day flying
the river wind, strong and smooth, played with me
willows murmured gently

at age 16 the kite took me
to a far-away city
longer and longer the string of the kite went
unaware
   it landed me on the other side of the earth

white clouds frolicked in the blue sky
near the green forests
red brick houses are aligned in rows
and roses send delicious fragrance to my senses

suddenly from the hills
a gentleman appeared
   broad chested
   with a big nose
"come to my home for some coffee, traveler"
   he said softly

i said yes . . .
it has been 30 years since!

today i am back
the same xiang river wind
the same willow trees
   murmuring
   "you're back"
the kite takes off
   unwilling to extend

you went to ames

i had known you for many months
seen you pass by with your long curly hair
    in your stylish coat
heard your friendly laughter and jokes
    from a distance

one day you invited me to your house
    for thanksgiving

five dogs were barking and running towards me
    as i entered your home

i met your mother
whose wrinkled face glowed, happily
i met your daughter
who was so beautiful that i thought i met an angel
you played with the dogs, talked about your dogs
and showed me pictures of your dogs
   and the dogs of your friends
   who shared the same dog fan list as you

and you told me the story of your life

your longing for a freer life and closer human contact
"with the advance of my age
i am no longer looking for a secluded family life
i am looking for a place more authentic than dc"
you said to me, the one who was enamored with the
cultural and political center that was dc

you cooked a delicious turkey for us all
and wrapped colorful cookies for me to take home

then one day you told me that you were going to ames
a city in middle america where more
   people liked to smile

the day before you left, you came to my house
   and found yourself amidst a feast and friends

the next day you went to ames
   and a part of me went
   quietly with you

magic food artist judy

in hollin hills where heritage glass houses stand
there lives a fair lady called judy
she prepares food like she's birthing flower blossoms
oh yes, we all know her
she's like a monarch butterfly turned magic food artist

her sunny and open kitchen is so large
It serves as a classroom
    where a dozen fit in to learn to cook
her living room is decorated
with original art works from around the world
music is played all day and heard
    in the rooms and hallway

judy twirls her magic fingers like wands
and creates exotic dishes so colorful
that you believe she picks rainbows from the clouds—
    italian, spanish, thai, mediterranean, new orleans
    chinese, mexican and indian, she does it all

melt-in-your-mouth gruyere cheese soufflé
scaloppini of salmon with hazelnuts
   and beurre blanc sauce
lemon zest rice pilaf
   and bittersweet chocolate mousse
   with crème chantilly swirls
   and chocolate espresso beans
names of dishes as enchanting as they taste

judy's signature sweetheart appetizer
has a nut splashed heart in the middle
the lovely heart blooms in white, yellow and red petals
the appetizer is so beautiful that you'd stare
   and forget to eat
   it's as succulent as her desserts
   like tiramisu parfaits

women and men, young and old
come here to learn to cook through private lessons
neighbors often pop in to see the new recipes
after a busy class
   they wine and dine on what they made
   for a full sit-down dinner
   at the yellow rose-adorned table

one day i visited judy after work
she lightly seared salmon, pinched arugula
   chopped tomatoes
and sprinkled marigold from her garden
"marigold is edible, you know"
voila, in minutes we started savoring the food

she sources herbs and vegetables from her garden
where monarchs, cardinals and deer visit often
she haunts ethnic stores and farms
   for fresh seafood, meats and unusual spices
"quality ingredients make quality food"

in hollin hills where heritage glass houses stand
there lives a fair lady called judy
she's like a monarch butterfly turned magic food artist
who has made a business teaching edible art
aroma lingers in the air long after each class

how do we learn?

by experience
said the pragmatist
through contact with events
we acquire knowledge or pain
to turn hate to love
we make friends with enemies
—how can we let our hearts bleed in vain?

by unlearning
said the zen master
through emptying our mind
we see things as they are
to turn hate to love
we become mindful
—where is the broken heart?

by truly being human
said the psychiatrist
through awakening the subconscious
we're millions of years in the making
to turn hate to love
we journey from murderers to heroes
—how can we evolve without sacrifice?

by connecting our brain neurons
said the modern neuroscientist
through only 21 days
we build a path of new neurons
to turn hate to love
break those damn pain neurons and
    forge ones with love!

solace

others seek happiness
i find solace in tears
knowing we all suffer
   comforts me

others seek fun
i find solace in boredom
repeating daily routines
   sustains me

others seek fortune
i find solace in misfortune
difficulties and losses
   strengthen me

others seek crowds
i find solace in solitude
being alone
   grounds me

3. loving

the heart opens

the heart opens
   yours and mine

a fountain of red springs
   sweeter than wine

each day waking up smiling
   away goes fear and we shine

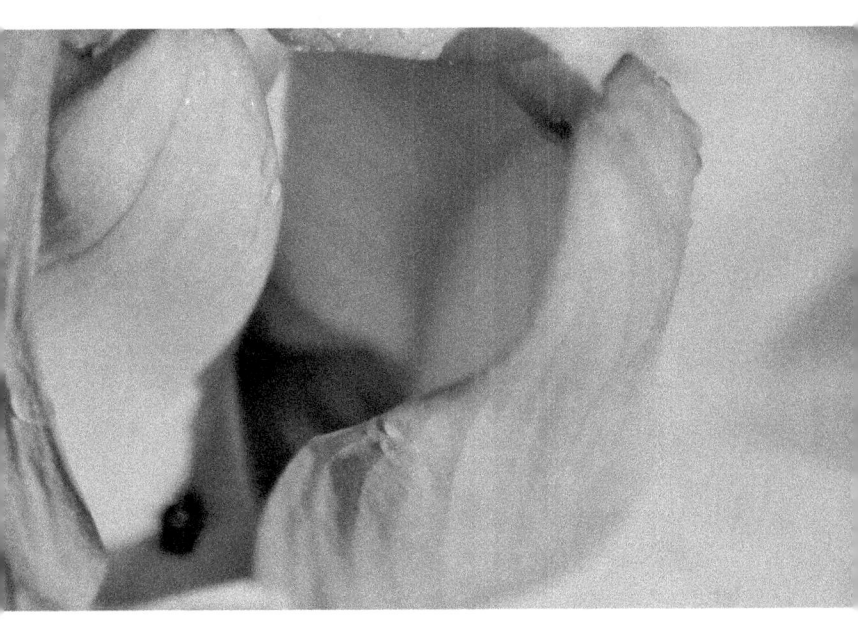

let me

before you take me, my dear
before you take me into your arms

let me look at you closely
in a hundred different ways
from dusk to dawn
awake or asleep
as the music flows

let me hold your hand freely
across the streets and meadows
like a little girl
who has not known the manners of the world

let me worship you piously
with flowers, smiles, tears and kisses
and say a thousand times
as if in a prayer
"i love you"

then only then
take me to your arms
   and bring me
   to bliss

our paris

you
initiated
me
into
a world
i never knew
existed
you set me
free
  by
    binding
      me

i
expand
and
tremble
in tantric
mystery
the mind
fires
the body
into
  a
    soulful
      dance

good morning, good night

good morning, good night
you are the first person i think of when i wake up
the last person i think about before i go to bed

good morning, good night
you are at my side when i cry
you are the reason behind my smile

good morning, good night
you inspire me to seek
truth, health and happiness

good morning, good night
you are my angel
you are my mate
you are my knight

till the sea's gone dry
and rocks melt with the sun
till i lie dying

good morning, good night

soulmates

we are soulmates
   made of the same material
i complete you
   and you me
one touch
   a world is created
   fountains, monuments, dotted trees
   birds chirping with ease

we are soulmates
   sung in the same tune
i flow in you
   and you me
one look
   the riddle is solved
paths open under our feet
   mirrors reveal ancient mysteries

we are soulmates
blessed by eternal parents
   of heaven and earth
wedded to the heartbeat
   of the universe

closer you come

closer you come
with deep-set eyes and chiseled features
from where the tigris and euphrates meet
mysterious women hide behind their veils
and pious men and women pray towards one direction
closer you come
accompanied by
   passionate persian waters

closer you come
with deep-set eyes and chiseled features
in your blood runs the ancient nile
in your veins sing the melodious quartets

in your mind are tuned open channels
closer you come
accompanied by
   the revolving statue of liberty

closer you come each day
crossing waters and mountains
opening doors and chambers
through the maze of electrons
   and the kaleidoscopic human heart

closer you come each day
   towards dawn, the yangtze, the potomac
   towards tomorrow...

a night of 100 kisses

on our river walk in the woods
you charmed me with many kisses
lips, necks, ears
eyes and cheeks
one, another and another
100 and more
while walking or standing
at dike marsh's overlooks
while resting on the bench
(ah, that gave you more opportunity)
and long and gentle kisses
while we lay down at the boat dock
earth as our bed
sky our net
clouds above carrying
our dream of 10,000 more kisses
   in the days ahead

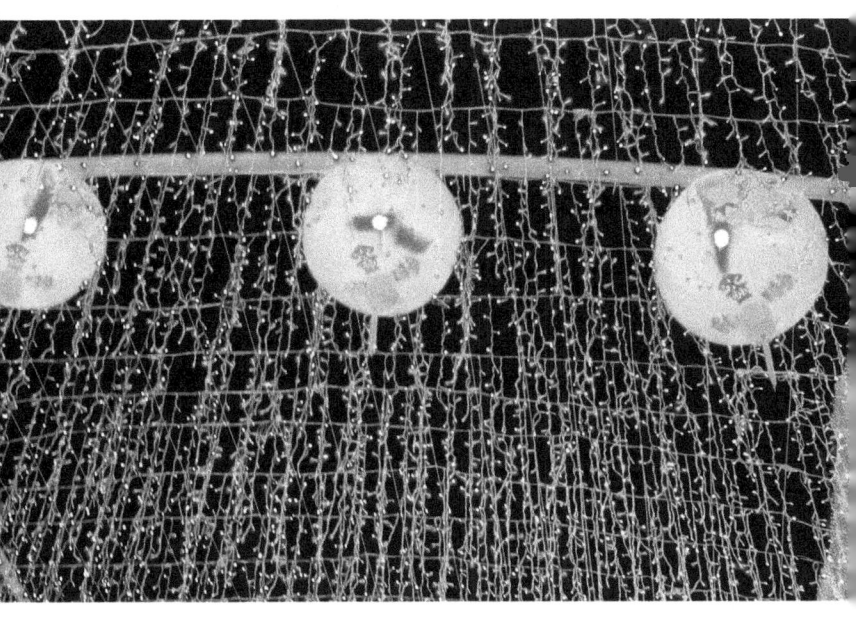

mom and dad

"how romantic
your dad still holds your mom's hands
—i saw them at their morning walk—
after 60 years"
i said
"she does not see clearly
he does not walk steadily"

our first valentine's

a flower paradise greeted me
at home after an 18-hour flight

roses, sunflowers, gladiolas
and little purple flowers with golden threads
expressing their full splendor
in glass vases and elephant stands

rejoicing
i unloaded my backpack
and touched the fresh petals
tracing their delicate lives

"wait a second"
you smiled like a magician
"there is something
we cannot miss"

you opened a box of cocoa truffles
and put one to my lips
and sealed the other end
with yours

chocolate melted slowly
blending our breath
the sweet aroma of
our first valentine's

is that you, my love?

i've been seeking
   in the misty mountains and crowded streets
   for you, my love

a man
- whose heart has carried the rose wreath and the cross
    - and known pain and ecstasy
- whose mind has wandered in the halls of knowledge
    - and known its limitations
- whose body and soul merged with mine
    - many lifetimes before
    - and is seeking again to join me

is that you, my love?

many men have come before you
- offering me their love
- with flowers, smiles and riches

when the veil was lifted, they became
- ghosts haunting the valleys of lust
    - leaving me wounded
    - bleeding on the floor

is that you, my love?
- the songs you sang to me
- the kisses you bestowed on me
- the heart image you drew with me
- and the hands that massaged my tired body to rest
- and the eyes that stared into my soul

is that you, my love?

waiting, arriving

i had been waiting in the silence of my heart
    for you to arrive for many, many centuries
a woman praying
    against the dark clouds of her times

i was a little six-year-old girl
    whose feet were bound for marriage prospects
i was the rich man's daughter
    who drowned herself to pursue her adolescent love
i was the slave's wife
    who was raped and thrown into the river
i was the burdened mother
    who died of childbirth in her young age
i was the single woman
    who imitated men and wanted nothing but her career

i was a woman
a woman waiting in the heart of darkness
    praying for the clouds to clear
a woman waiting, waiting for you to arrive

on a cloudless day
across the majestic sky
    with open arms, you arrived
you stood in front of me
    looking deep into my eyes—
    you heard my prayers

the gates of our hearts flung open
joy overflowed
   within us and between us and around us
a woman and a man
ready to receive each other as equals
   in the heart of the universe
   between the monuments
   of time

love promise

i made a promise
to myself
to love you
till the last ray of my sunset—

you, a hyperactive mind
an aging body
and a fragile soul
just like myself

i'm keeping my promise
with this love poem
and a daily omelet
i share with you

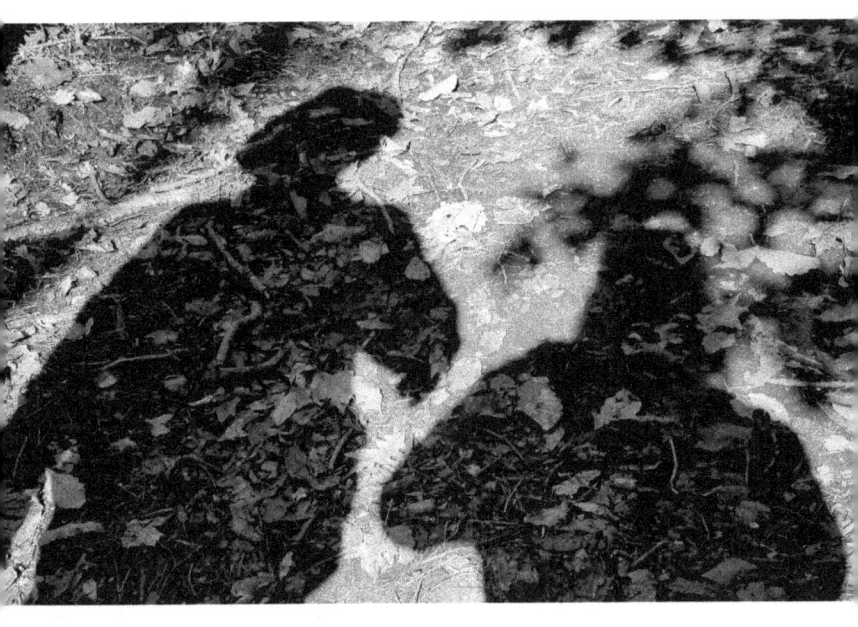

4. seeing

悟

petals of the soul

you saw me
i saw you
   in the hustling bustling city

memories
   of the far-away place
   awoke

petals of the soul

soul song

3am in a southern china city by the sea
in a minibus with my qigong teacher in 1986
after a healing session with a troubled student
we were on our way to the hotel suite

humming a tune half aware
i stared at the passing trees
suddenly the grass begins to move
   trees become alive and the sky
    is opening up, connecting the ocean
    —waves widening
   until the entire universe is singing the tune
i disappeared into the song, unaware of the bus
i had never heard the song but i knew every note

since then, i've become a singer
i sing when i walk on the streets
   or drive on highways
i sing when i'm overburdened
i sing when i'm down
in the song, i laugh, cry and fly
in the song, i travel space and time

the song, like lotus petals on the path
   leads me to an inspired life!

in spirit

when i am one, i am spirit
i walk, talk and love in spirit
what's essential is invisible

i see with my inner eye
trees mated to the earth
rivers flow in full force
nurturing plants and places along their path
and slowly decomposing debris and logs

the earth contains and digests it all
silently in its revolving hearth

when i am one, i am spirit
trees, rivers and earth are
in spirit

balanced

lotus effect

rising

from a muddy pond
like a queen clad in green silk

morning dewdrops
roll gently on your face
in the breeze

cleansing
glistening
until you illuminate
   again

a canopy for the lotus

A lotus leaf has an amazing self-cleaning property due to the nanoscopic architecture on its surface. Water droplets fallen on the leaf will roll off, taking along with them the dust and dirt particles. Lotus rising out of muddy water is commonly used as an analogy for self-cultivation in asian traditions.

the invisible S in yin yang

hidden in the middle between yin and yang
   is the S
in perpetual transformation
nurturing and releasing

like the mists rising from the rivers
sending the scent of pine into the air
the path winds from the foot of the mountains
   to the temple on top

within the circle
yin resides in yang; yang resides in yin
stillness in motion; feminine in masculine
   like winter buries fertile soil for spring

yin yang gives birth to five elements
metal, wood, water, fire and earth
then captured in eight trigrams and more hexagrams
an intricate cosmic web of energy forms

one and many
move us in ten directions
   as the ever-balancing S
codes wisdom in our consciousness

one minute

if the world stops completely
i mean stops completely
and gives you one minute
    and a superpower in that minute
what would your superpower be?

"i'd save my baby from suffocation
    in the car when i was on drugs"
"i'd return the million-dollar diamond ring
    i stole from my best friend"
"i'd tell the man i've avoided for years that i loved him"
"i'd kill my uncle who raped my mom"
"i'd stalk my dad who deserted us"
"i'd stop my family from feuding
    about hillary or trump"
"i'd send flowers to my ex whom
    i abused for many years"
"i'd feed all the starving children"

you've not spoken
what would your minute be?
"i will close my eyes and savor the moment
    the world is now finally at peace
    even for just one minute!"

i thought i was

i thought
i was enlightened
when you rejected my view
i felt crushed

i thought
i was kind
when you hurt me
i wanted to hurt you back

i thought
i was generous
when your ex came here
i wanted her to vanish

i thought
i was strong
when you told me of your problems with your kids
i wanted to run

i thought
i was

queen or me?

one night i dreamed
i was the queen who ruled over england
presiding over a ceremony—

her solemn look
fancy hat
and a properly positioned power entourage

when i woke up
i was puzzled

did i dream i was the queen
or did the queen dream she was me
living an ordinary woman's life?

a cup of tea at starbucks
an ice cream cone at häagen-dazs
and a moonlit walk on the streets with my love

visiting historic staunton

on a spring weekend i escaped to the mountains
accompanied by my partner
   a diplomat in war-torn states

we set out friday afternoon in a car
   and arrived in a small town called staunton
   flanked by peaceful mountain ranges
   george washington national forests
   and the shenandoah

the place we stayed
   seemed to come out of a sci-fi movie
   a resort-like psychiatric hospital turned prison
   now a heritage hotel

shakespeare was waiting for us in the replica
   of a 16th century playhouse
on the stage, falstaff strutted his big belly
   in and out of treasure hunts

across the open parking garage, the flour mill wheel
   blazes in the sun
water still runs under the metal bridge

not far stands president wilson's birth house
hailed as a homecoming boy
   wilson visited the town as president-elect
did virginian mountains come to him
   when he declared war to end all wars?

laughing santa and buddha

santa
"hohoho"
buddha
"hahaha"
huge bellies
carrying
   laughter

bringing
gifts and joy
to billions
on family mantelpieces and altars
like comforting pain medicine
   from the counter

"see, their bellies shake
hahaha
hohoho"
laughed my 5-year-old
"i tickled them—
   grandpa santa and buddha"

NICE

金玉滿堂

TO DO LIST

• PAcK sleigh
• wrap present
• CALL Mrs. CLAUS

starry night sky

sunday night
chincoteague park refuge
the lighthouse
shone its light far around us
leaving behind the city noise

crickets were singing
wolves howling it seems
we stood at the bridge
between the city and refuge

as i raised my head to kiss you
i saw the stars
so many in the night sky
larger, smaller, blinking, fleeting
i have forgotten how beautiful they are

the same stars
i saw when i was little
and before i moved to the big cities
   yet they've always been there
   always every night

my last trip

i've dreamed of the ocean
today

standing here
my last trip of 91 years

the sunset paints all
in red and orange canopy

disappearing
in the distance

children build sand domes
lovers walk in pairs

atlantic ocean!

i've loved and lost
i've suffered and lived

now i am ready
   take me
     dissolve me in your glory!

5. returning

歸

the ring

the tai chi symbol necklace
stares at me—black and white eyes
from the small velvet trellis
   of the jewelry stand at the tao healing conference

reminds me of the universal energy ring
i bought here last year
the ring showed twirling circles
signifying connectedness of all in the universe
   artistically crafted by master nan lu's teacher

"you know
i lost the ring on one of my travels"
i raised my bare fingers
   my face touched by regrets

"oh, dear
so you gave it away to the universe
someone else now has the gift"
   smiled the tao jewelry seller

"that is beautiful—
my gift to the world"
a knot in me opened
i laughed
   the ring is living its own life!

the eyes of the tai chi symbol
blinked a little
   as if in accord

secret code

greek philosophers say the world is
composed of four elements
   earth, water, air and fire
chinese thinkers say the world is
made up of wuxin, or five elements
   metal, wood, water, fire and earth

quantum physicists believe
the universe is mysteriously bound
by atoms and subatomic particles
like a gigantic bowl
   of quantum gumbo soup!

if we are all energy
what makes us organically beautiful?
instagram selfies, luxury clothes and sexy figures?
what makes us organically powerful?
physical strength, piles of money
   and millions of twitter followers?
what makes us organically happy?
loud laughs, constant highs, numerous lovers?

is there a secret code behind all things?
"mountains are mountains, rivers are rivers
mountains are not mountains, rivers are not rivers
mountains are just mountains, rivers are just rivers"
said the zen master

forget the riddles
do not mention the classics

a mountain stream flows into the ocean
a music note is most pleasant to the ear
when in concert with others
we feel most vibrant
when in harmony with ourselves
and with the world

ah-ha, isn't "harmony" the code!

circles of harmony

life is full of confusing shapes
until we've learned to
draw circles
   from within ourselves—
   our own life force

each of us is an energetic system
affecting and affected by those around us
our health depends on
the balance of yin yang principles
and the harmony of five elements
   metal, wood, water, fire and earth
   within us and around us

within us plays the alchemy of the elements
around us performs the symphony of collective battles

a good doctor is wise
who knows you and herself
she does not let your symptoms trick her
from curing you of a disease
she finds the root cause
   and teaches you to self-heal

you will become a doctor yourself
because your body
is your own carrier
your emotions, thoughts and lifestyle
   are more important than your pills

be still
listen to your body as the body never lies
open the gateways
harmonize the elements
charge up the energy channels
those meridian rivers that run through your organs
connect the water in you
connect the fire in you
connect the earth in you

draw circles every morning
invite joy and love into your circles
release anger and anxiety
life is not an accident
there are no accidents
those are not mistakes
go with the flow
begin your dance

dance in circles of harmony
when harmony is achieved
the body will heal itself

dance dance dance

This poem was inspired by the teachings of Dr. Nan Lu, a Traditional Chinese Medicine doctor and martial artist, who practices in New York.

full moon night

on a full moon night
i cradled my heart in my hands
looking for those i loved when i was young
my grandma, my mom and sister
and the boy who shared my school desk

my grandma has departed
my mom still enjoys good health
my sister is busy with her kids and grandkids
and the boy—i do not know what he's become

i cradled my heart in my hands
standing on the earth's western hemisphere
the red soil has turned to yellow and grey
my neighbors enjoy neon lights more than the moon
and my husband favors mooncakes more than the moon

the full moon
holding my heart on a string
travels the globe, west and east
the moon in my adopted land shines as full as
   in my hometown!

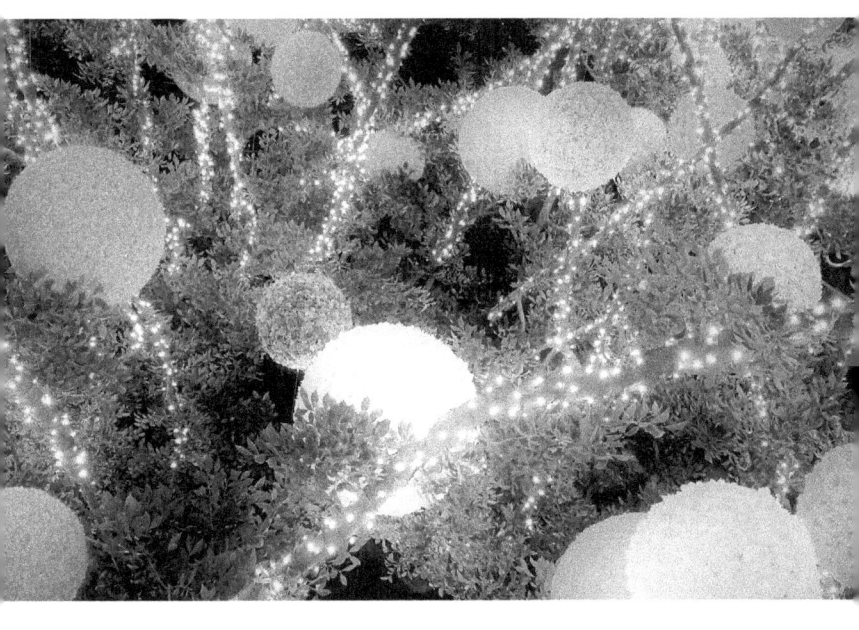

a new day

a crimson ribbon across the sky
   unveils another morning
white clouds float
   erasing the memories of yesterday's storms

old questions remain
   echoed in the bamboo bent low from the rough winds

"should we choose
   flowers that will fade
   or lasting evergreens?

do we live to take more breath
   or die for what takes our breath away?"

bamboo shakes off the morning dew, bent yet dignified
   "flowers and evergreens are seasons' different clothes
   why one or the other?"

secret symphony at our birth

the universe is a symphony of vibrations
played by planets and stars
in their endless orbits
to the elements of fire, water, air and earth
   for beings at birth

most however are unaware

you have more fire
i have more water
he has more earth
she has more air

you are courageous but impatient
i am considerate but manipulative
he is practical but slow
she is intelligent but unsteady

most however are unaware

we capture 12 months in 365 days
and hours, minutes and seconds
plus north and south, east and west
in our space-time continuum
each of us takes on multiple combinations at birth
that makes us each unique
   that could be a superpower given at birth

i was born aries sun
aries moon
leo mars
aquarius venus
my sun trines my mars
my sun conjuncts my jupiter and mercury
my pluto conjuncts my ascendant

thus i am passionate, impatient
witty and caring
loyal and jealous
i probe deep into the mysteries of things
(that could be my superpower)

what vibrations were you endowed with
   at the time of your birth?
what are the positions of your sun, moon,
   venus and mars?
do you know your hidden superpower?

i'm full

i'm full
for i've known
the violation of my heart by abusive powers
the trampling of my body by heavy boots
the suffocation of my soul by ignorance

i'm full
for i've felt
my parents and grandparents
my sons and daughters
hurt in my own hands and almost nullified

i'm full
for i've heard
day and night through the thick walls
the desperate cries of my neighbors
their tears swelling up old rivers

i'm full
for i've seen
the last bowl of rice
the last ray of light on earth
about to be destroyed

i've learned to be full
pregnant each moment
   with a new dawn

the ficus tree

"that tree has been there for 49 years
it was a gift on our wedding day"
said kathy, jake's elder sister
the oldest of 11 siblings
her eyes glittered on her time-worn face

"it was so small
over the years it just grew
the leaves are abundant all year around
i did not know i had a green thumb
i take it out to the yard each summer

when i moved it in this fall
i had to cut some branches
to fit in the dining room"
her husband nodded
"the tree has added so much to our lives"

i looked at the full thanksgiving dinner table
kathy's son and his family, who are local to washington
a cousin and his wife, their daughter
   and her arab husband
   two playful grand-twins
jake, myself and a long-time friend

across from the dining room
was a piano with pictures
of their daughter, who lives in brooklyn
a second son, who lives in italy
and a decorative pumpkin
   next to a heart-shaped wreath

a river spirit in bliss

you went suddenly, without a word
days, hours, minutes and more days

i could no longer see your loving face
so vibrant and serene
i could no longer visit you at your elegant home
talking about anything and everything
i could no longer call to hear you laugh
while driving on dc's congested roads

you went suddenly—without a word
days, weeks and soon to be months
yet you left me so much
the spirit to achieve and always improve
10,000 details to look over
many memories of joy and meaningful work
two decades of friendship
and a riverside home with glorious views

i did not know such grace, such love
until you came to visit again

a small figure draped in silk
over the river, the trees and peonies
quietly in the moonlight
across our window
   a river spirit in bliss

separation

our greatest pain is separation
separation from our mothers
from our hometowns, our loved ones
   and from our own hearts

innocence is lost
love turns into hate
joy gives way to sorrow
   and wars and madness never cease

our greatest joy also comes from separation
because of separation
there is the individual life
your life, my life, his and her life

struggle for freedom
sacrifice for future rewards
animals, plants and flowers
   in never-ending cycles

between pain and joy spring forth
god, allah, buddha,
   and the oneness
      with it all

let us celebrate one another

look into my eyes
blue green brown black
   blue as the ocean
   green the pines
   brown the earth
   black the rock

go deeper
you will see the rise of a young tree
   the breath of a baby
   and the power of an elephant

the red heart beats
within me
in the same rhythm
as those around me
   tick tick tick
   a hidden stream linking us each

under the blazing sun
and the silvery moon
i test my wings for flying
   and manifest my being

white light
opens the channels
to the ancient rivers
millions of years in the making
   of the human race

we suffer
we endure
we suffer more
we endure more

we become self-conscious
why why why
are we born good or evil

adam and eve
driven out of
the walled garden for eating the apple
confess your sins
or wear the scarlet letter on your chest

a straw-hatted old man
fishing alone in the cold river snow
no birds or human in view
follow the laws of nature
or wander forever in your own homes

we make love and wars
kill thousands with our hands and swords
   and atomic bombs
caring less for millions who are starving
sick and wounded, with little support

happiness or meaning
i choose the latter
i am no tragic hero
molding and creating
i sacrifice for tomorrow

christmas and new year's again

run run run
run to the top of the shining hill
decorate the tree
light the fireworks
let us celebrate
let us embrace each other
   our colored eyes
   our red hearts

let us celebrate one another

into the distance i walk

on my way to work i stopped
    for a walk in the woods
the 50th time when the sun returned
    to the place of my birth

the light shines through snowflakes
    mixing ice with earth
the gravel road circles the island
    running across marshes

i walk
    amidst glistening trees
    melting wetlands
    and slanting grass
i walk

birth and death but a moment's breath
    in these deep woods
love and hate but a thought in a breeze
    in these deep woods

now and before the island stands

into the distance i walk

DEDICATION

|
|

my

deep

gratitude

goes to those

who've enlightened me

on the path to compassion and

wisdom through their presence and teachings

like beautiful lanterns

renhui
("ren" = benevolent; "hui" = wisdom)

仁
慧

Afterword

Song of a Lotus Leaf
My Dao Journey in Poetry

*The following article is published in the
"Journal of Daoist Studies" (Volume 14, 2021).
Except the three images, all content is kept the same. To get a copy of
the journal, please visit https://uhpress.hawaii.edu/title/jds.*

It is not often that a poet gets the chance to introduce her poems in an academic journal. While appreciating this opportunity, I ask myself the question: What do readers want to know most from the poet herself? Do they want to know the intended meanings hidden in the writing of her poems, or perhaps the life experiences behind them?

Song of a Lotus Leaf is a collection of poems I wrote in my journal over many years as I went through life. I have taken poetic license for some of the specifics, yet maintained a laser focus on retaining the essence of my writing. My life is representative of a new generation of people who have lived between two cultures. In this point in my life, my experience has been split almost equally between my first 25 years in China and the last 25 years in America. My life philosophy was formed during my early years in China, while most of my adult life experiences have been encountered in America.

As the poems collected in this book were written during the most recent twenty years of my life, many poems are relevant to the American immigrant as well as the Daoist student. Struggles such as homesickness, loss of love, divorce, challenging adjustments to new value systems, financial constraints, and subsequent emotional breakdowns were all thrown on my path. Miraculously, awakening occurred at the same time on different levels in my body, mind, and spirit. These poems are the evidence of those awakenings, and the accompanying photos serve as further documentation of those experiences.

These poems are the result of inward reflection, spoken in a simple, meditative, and authentic voice, with minimum punctuation and all in lower case, such as in the following from a poem called "Circles of Harmony."

life is full of confusing shapes
until we've learned to
draw circles
   from within ourselves—
   our own life force

each of us is an energetic system
affecting and affected by those around us
our health depends on
the balance of yin yang principles
and the harmony of five elements
   metal, wood, water, fire and earth
   within us and around us

within us plays the alchemy of the elements (p. 114)

A hundred years from now, my life might be an interesting case study of an individual who grew up with the

Daoist teachings of living close to nature and later being transplanted into a culture that has much less dependency on nature.

My Dao Journey

My encounter with Daoism came when I sought to restore my health because I was sick with insomnia and a stomach problem. This occurred while I was studying Western literature in China in 1986, and it led me to an energy-healing workshop where I first learned qigong. My health was restored miraculously in just a couple of weeks. This amazing result piqued my interest. I became fascinated with qigong and in due course also with taijiquan and acupuncture.

This fascination eventually led me to Daoism because it is the philosophical basis for those practices. I kowtowed to my qigong master and the taiji master who followed, eventually engaging myself in an acupuncture program. During this same period, I frequented temples and studied meditation, Daoism, Zen, and Buddhism to learn the collective traditions—receiving the name Renhui 仁慧 (Benevolent Wisdom) in a Beijing temple.

After years of reading and practicing energy healing, my eyes were opened to the Daoist philosophical basis behind classical Chinese art forms—from Tang poetry, landscape painting, calligraphy, martial arts, and Fengshui to the cosmology of the *Yijing*. The creativity hidden behind qigong is present in every art form and at the center of each is the Dao principle.

I carried my enthusiasm with me when I arrived in Washington, DC, to work in a doctorate program at George Washington University. My understanding of Dao made it possible for me to look at modern writings by Western giants such as W. Somerset Maugham, Emily Dickenson, Ralph Waldo Emerson, Willa Cather, Wallace Stevens, Ezra Pound, and Charles Baudelaire in a new light. I saw their existential struggles, their creative sparks, and their influences by Eastern philosophies and religions. My new insight inspired me to study the work of T. S. Eliot. In fact, I even wrote my dissertation on Eliot's source and path of creativity in the context of Buddhist meditation on death, which was well received among the professors of Western and Eastern literature and religions at the university.

Five Stages

The Dao journey in my poetic "memoir" follows a linear progression. The five chapters of *Song of the Lotus Leaf* match the five stages of my personal growth: suffering, creating, loving, seeing, and returning. Suffering opens the book with poems about the painful experiences in life that eventually birthed my spiritual and emotional awakening. The act of creating something was instrumental in healing the pain, whether it was explored through taiji, meditation, imitating nature, singing, painting, stone house building, cooking, learning, or poetry writing. Love heals the spirit further through romance, friendship, and emotional insights. The act of seeing moves the self through the dimensions of the existence—from the individual to the collective, to nature, and to the cosmos.

The final stage, returning, illuminates how transformative power is embedded in the cycle of life and that harmony is the "Secret Code" of everything.

a mountain stream flows into the ocean
a music note is most pleasant to the ear
when in concert with others
we feel most vibrant
when in harmony with ourselves
and with the world

ah-ha, isn't "harmony" the code! (p. 113)

The character for Dao 道 shows a path in the left quadrant and of a head on the right side. Simply put, the relationship between the components within the word Dao can be interpreted as "someone is walking". Dao also means to know, or to follow a method or technique. It is a noun, a verb, an adjective, and even a measure unit!

My Dao journey is also epiphanic and transformational, just as in sudden flash of insight within the Zen tradition. These "light bulb" moments are Oneness moments achieved through meditation when the body is relaxed and the mind is emptied. Zen wisdom is a combination of Daoism and Buddhism. The character for Zen, *chan* 禪, shows piety on the left side and simplicity on the right.

The following poem "Soul Song" depicts the moment when I first experienced Oneness:

suddenly the grass begins to move
   trees become alive and the sky
   is opening up, connecting the ocean
   —waves widening
   until the entire universe is singing the tune
i disappeared into the song, unaware of the bus
i had never heard the song but i knew every note (p. 86)

The poem that best describes a Dao path is "The Invisible S in Yin Yang." It elucidates the flow in the yin yang symbol. The poem zooms in on the S-shaped line where yin and yang are connected within the symbol and creates an actual path, like a Chinese landscape painting.

The poem then moves to the abstract again to describe what yin yang principles are and how they bring us wisdom. Here is the entire poem.

hidden in the middle between yin and yang
   is the S
in perpetual transformation
nurturing and releasing

like the mists rising from the rivers
sending the scent of pine into the air
the path winds from the foot of the mountains
   to the temple on top

within the circle
yin resides in yang; yang resides in yin

stillness in motion; feminine in masculine
   like winter buries fertile soil for spring

yin yang gives birth to five elements
metal, wood, water, fire, and earth
then captured in eight trigrams and more hexagrams
an intricate cosmic web of energy forms

one and many
move us in ten directions
   as the ever-balancing S
codes wisdom in our consciousness (p. 92)

Stage 1: Suffering—Awakening to the Darkness

The stage of suffering *(ku* 苦) covers different types of pain: homesickness in a foreign country, emotional pain due to being misunderstood and abandoned, stress from too many choices, bone-breaking physical agony, the rational college educational system that lacks heart and soul, and racial and ideological warfare.

"I Am Dawn," the first poem of the book is about the suffering of personal growth. I use "dawn" as a metaphor for myself. Dawn emerges after night to shine light on the earth, similar to how I came to experience light and the intention to serve others after a dark period in my life.

i am dawn
i carry the promise of your day
   when you get up from your bed
and walk upright

>   into the shimmering glow
>   to work, love, fight and play
>
> i am dawn
> i survived a deadly storm
>   where seafarers were lost at sea
>   and seagulls wailed
>   through a darkly night
>
> from the heart of darkness
>   i was born (p. 2)

The last two lines are reminiscent of the words in the *Daode jing* on how darkness is the "gateway" to all things. While dawn is clearly associated with the poet, it can also be poetry itself, since poetry comes to us from the darkness of imagination.

"Your Visit," is a poem about the sadness I felt due to the long separation from my birth country. As my friend was telling stories of China, my heart rushed like the currents of the Yangtze River, where I grew up: "you turned into my river / resonated with the voice of my mother / i cried" (p. 11).

"Fateful Night" is about a painful moment in my marriage. One night, I fell to the floor in despair. As the moon reminded me of home and hope, "I rose." I, as the subject, made it happen. The act of becoming my own rose is buried in the potential of these two words.

> that fateful night
> i fell from my bed
>   to the floor...

i couldn't get up
he was again at his video games
   dead as hell . . .
i saw on my chest
   threads of moonlight—
   the scent of home
i rose (p. 4)

The poem echoes the work of the famous Tang poet Li Bo, "Quiet Night Thoughts." The bright moon reminds the poet of his longing for home during the Mid-Autumn Festival when families gather under the full moon to eat mooncakes. It says:

> *At the foot of my bed bright moonlight*
> *Like frost gleaming on the floor*
> *I lift my head to gaze at the moon*
> *Lowering my head I think of home*

Following this are poems about the pain of living in the U.S. "Remembering Mr. Poe" touches upon the American habit of setting aside only one day—Halloween—to ponder the dark side of life and see the light within it. The dark and unknown side as a critical component of reality is normally rejected as useless and unimportant under American pragmatism. Thus, this unbalanced perspective produces the depression that permeates the daily lives of many Americans.

"Stress Made in America" is about a stressed-out young college graduate living a busy life while burdened by many responsibilities. Life becomes a set of rational choices and tasks devoid of pleasure.

"Come Back to Me, Heart" criticizes the academic rule of objectivity where the mind reigns and the heart is completely ignored. People who live in these environments are out of balance, thus causing suffering in their individual lives as well as in society as a whole.

Stage 2: Creating—Following Natural Laws

The Chinese term *wuwei* 無為 (nonaction) does not mean to do nothing; it means to do things following natural laws without human meddling. When we perform work according to the laws, the Dao is manifested. Chinese civilization has emphasized the perfection of a craft following its natural laws. This is so important to Daoist philosophy that the word *chuang* 創 depicts a knife in the right side of the written character, portraying the act of creating.

This section of the book opens with a poem about the practice and wisdom of *taiji*. "Daily Earth Wisdom Routine" describes inner alignment that builds up an external alignment with nature:

stand upright
be rooted like a tree

string an invisible thread
   above your head from the sky
and close your eyes
relax all joints and muscles
quiet your mind
let a column of white light
pour in from the top of your head
   to under your feet
feel the connection
   above and below and all around
feel the suppleness
   within
breathe in the tall pines
breathe in the fresh bamboo grove
breathe in the misty mountain air
one minute
two minutes
fifteen minutes
then tai chi
365 days (p. 30)

The poem "Connect" further shows us to restore balance, we must learn from nature.

"connect
   with each step you take
   the feet rooted into the ground
      deep like me, the tree
   the head aligned to me, the sky
      as if lifted by a thread
   the trunk centered and upright

> yet flexible like me, the river
> and the whole body relaxed
> connected to me, the earth" (p. 32)

Creative efforts come from the desire for self-expression. What is the purpose of life? How do we overcome pain and transcend our limitations? The creative works highlighted in this section include aspects of myself expressed as an artist, a gardener, a poet, a resort house builder, a chef, etc. Each self in its identity of expression connects with its creative impulse and produces something of beauty. The artist in the poem "Rainbow Wind" uses color and lines as tools of self-expression. Her work connects her with the energy the object emits.

> rivers bleed through it all in gold
>   breaking pain into joy (p. 34)

This abstract art seems to perform an alchemy with water, shattering painful feelings to release joy. Nature in Classical Daoist poetry is imbued with symbolic meaning. Daoists and Zen masters believe nature is the best artist and humans are imitators of nature. Here is "How Do We Learn?"

> by unlearning
> said the zen master
> through emptying our mind
> we see things as they are
> to turn hate to love
> we become mindful
> —where is the broken heart? (p. 52)

Stage 3: Loving—Leading a Heart-Centered Life

The heart, from the traditional Chinese perspective, is responsible for our spiritual and mental activities, the location where the spirit (*shen* 神) resides. The Chinese word for love *(ai* 愛) is illuminating, showing the symbol for friendship plus a heart. The character for the word "enlightenment" *(wu* 悟), similarly is composed of a heart on the left and the ancient word for "I" on the right. It shows being fully oneself from the depth of one's heart.

The modern world is marked by a mobile lifestyle. We move every few years to a new job or home, and even friendships and romantic relationships are hard to maintain for long. Like many of her peers, the poet has experienced tragedy in the domain of the heart. The chapter begins with "The Heart Opens":

the heart opens
  yours and mine

a fountain of red springs
  sweeter than wine

each day waking up smiling
  away goes fear and we shine (p. 58)

Part of the Great One, we are all connected. The heart is the center of connection for each individual. When we open our hearts, we accept each other as is. Romantic love without compassion will end in divorce. Friendship without soulful connection will not last. Yin and yang can be two lovers and two friends. These closely related pairs are connected by the heart and soul, not just the physical body or mutual hobbies.

"A Night of 100 Kisses" celebrates the joy of being connected to a fellow being who also loves nature.

on our river walk in the woods
   you charmed me with many kisses
   lips, necks, ears
   eyes and cheeks
   one, another and another...
   our dream of 10,000 more kisses
      in the days ahead (p. 70)

"Soulmates" shows just how deeply connected we are:

we are soulmates
blessed by eternal parents
   of heaven and earth
wedded to the heartbeat
   of the universe (p. 66)

"Mom and Dad" is a testimony of a lifetime union:

"how romantic
your dad still holds your mom's hands
—i saw them at their morning walk—
after 60 years"
i said
"she does not see clearly
he does not walk steadily" (p. 72)

In "Is That You, My Love?" the poet seeks permanence of love:

i've been seeking
>   in the misty mountains and crowded streets
>   for you, my love

a man
>   whose heart has carried the rose wreath and the cross
>   and known pain and ecstasy
>   whose mind has wandered in the halls of knowledge
>   and known its limitations
>   whose body and soul merged with mine
>   many lifetimes before
>   and is seeking again to join me (p. 76)

Here the poet seeks a relationship she has had with the same person for many lifetimes—mature and balanced, not restricted by reason. Immortality is hinted at but the dream is to have a love relationship that can last in the same way that yin and yang are paired for eternity.

Stage 4: Seeing—The Larger Perspective

In healing through living a heart-centered life, our perspective moves into the larger world, like the bird's-eye view in a landscape painting with layers of mountains beyond the mists, and clouds, and rivers winding through a valley. It leads to an understanding on an intuitive level.

"The Invisible S in Yin Yang" focuses on the middle line in the shape of S in the yin yang diagram. Most people only see the two forces and their interdependent relationship. They do not see that the curving line in the middle symbolizes eternal change, denoting transformation in a perpetual state towards perfect balance. Transformation is central to Daoist cosmology; all phenomena are the transformations of the One and they are in constant change. The One gives birth to the two and then three, indicating the infinite multitude of everything of the One.

one and many
move us in ten directions
   as the ever-balancing S
codes wisdom in our consciousness (p. 92)

The One and the many exist on the same cosmic plane. The movement toward balance teaches us the way.

Another poem that illustrates the principle of transformation is "Queen or Me?" It relates to the sense of "other," seen as an illusion in Daoism where the cosmos is a unity and was inspired by Zhuangzi's famous "Butterfly Dream."

i was the queen who ruled over england
presiding over a ceremony—

. . .

when i woke up
i was puzzled

did i dream i was the queen
or did the queen dream she was me
living an ordinary woman's life? (p. 98)

Next, "Soul Song" describes the mystical experience I had during the time when I first practiced qigong in a city in Southern China. The unity of my surroundings merged into a song at that time. I was singing the Western song "Memories" when it happened. Since then, the world I experience is no longer centered on my smaller self: "The natural world is alive in unison ... the song, like lotus petals on the path /leads me to an inspired life!" (p. 86)

"One Minute" imagines what people would confess if they were given a superpower for a moment. Each wishes to turn back time when tragedy occurs. There is a sage who wants peace, realizing how much conflict the world has.

you've not spoken
what would your minute be?
"i will close my eyes and savor the moment
   the world is now finally at peace
   even for just one minute!" (p. 94)

"Separation," finally, expresses the paradoxical view that sorrow and joy are both the result of separation. Religions of the world are all responses to this paradox.

our greatest pain is separation
separation from our mothers
from our hometowns, our loved ones
   and from our own hearts

innocence is lost
love turns into hate
joy gives way to sorrow
   and wars and madness never cease

our greatest joy also comes from separation
because of separation

there is the individual life
your life, my life, his and her life

struggle for freedom
sacrifice for future rewards
animals, plants and flowers
   in never-ending cycles

between pain and joy spring forth
god, allah, buddha,
   and the oneness
      with it all (p. 130)

Stage 5: Returning—Homecoming

Life is a cycle, resulting ultimately in homecoming *(gui* 歸*)*. According to Daoism, during and after the ups and downs of life, we are pulled to return to the source where our true nature shines—simple, pure, and in alignment with the original creative energy *(yuanqi* 元氣*)*. "Circles of Harmony" describes the process of returning to our true nature:

be still
listen to your body as the body never lies
open the gateways
harmonize the elements
charge up the energy channels
those meridian rivers that run through your organs
connect the water in you
connect the fire in you
connect the earth in you

draw circles every morning
invite joy and love into your circles
release anger and anxiety
life is not an accident
there are no accidents
those are not mistakes
go with the flow
begin your dance

dance in circles of harmony
   when harmony is achieved
   the body will heal itself (p. 116)

There are no accidents. Most of us may not know why but the why is embedded in the process—the way of the Dao.

    The process of returning, moreover, is to merge, not to divide. Choices are futile. "A New Day" expresses choices in terms of fading flowers and lasting evergreens. It is the human mind that gives them different value. They co-exist and have equal value in nature.

"should we choose
>   flowers that will fade
>   or lasting evergreens?

do we live to take more breath
>   or die for what takes our breath away?"

bamboo shakes off the morning dew, bent yet dignified
>   "flowers and evergreens are seasons' different
clothes
>   why one or the other?"(p. 120)

"Let Us Celebrate One Another" relates to transformative people and their lives. We are different races and species, yet we are from the same source and are embedded in the *yuanqi*, which created each life.

look into my eyes
blue green brown black
>   blue as the ocean
>   green the pines
>   brown the earth
>   black the rock

go deeper
you will see the rise of a young tree
>   the breath of a baby
>   and the power of an elephant

the red heart beats
within me
in the same rhythm
as those around me

    tick tick tick
    a hidden stream linking us each (p. 132)

In my eyes are other people's eyes—black, brown, blue. In my eyes are trees and elephants. We inhale the oxygen exhaled by trees. We are One in the large scheme of things, transforming and transformative within.

    Like most Asians, my most favorite activity is walking in nature, so it is not surprising that the last poem was inspired by walking in the woods. On my 50th birthday, I walked the trail of Roosevelt Island and had an epiphany, expressed in "Into the Distance I Walk"

on my way to work i stopped
    for a walk in the woods
the 50th time when the sun returned
    to the place of my birth

the light shines through snowflakes
    mixing ice with earth
the gravel road circles the island
    running across marshes

i walk
    amidst glistening trees
    melting wetlands
    and slanting grass
i walk

birth and death but a moment's breath
    in these deep woods
love and hate but a thought in a breeze
    in these deep woods

now and before the island stands

into the distance i walk (p. 136)

As both sun and snowflakes settled on me, illuminating the path and eliminating the path at the same time, I felt the fleeting nature of my body and the permanence of the island.

My shadow becomes smaller and smaller against the island; the self becomes a dot in space and time. This dot no longer possesses individual consciousness and that is what a Dao journey is—from self to selflessness. A life serves a purpose and then passes on to nourish future life. The image is the same as one portrayed in a Daoist landscape painting that illustrates a small group of sages drinking tea along a winding path in the mountains, shrouded by the white mists rising from the river that flows nearby, becoming at one with nature.

Conclusion

Self-cultivation, inward looking, spiritual awakening, enlightenment, and more all are components of this collection. Although it covers two decades for the poet, it is a path many before her have traveled—sages and seekers of the Dao alike. While set mostly in the U.S., China is the subtext. The poet finally transforms into a "lotus leaf" rising from the muddy pond of life and serving as a protector of lotus, as described in "Lotus Effect":

rising

from a muddy pond
like a queen clad in green silk

morning dewdrops
roll gently on your face
in the breeze

cleansing
glistening
until you illuminate
   again

a canopy for the lotus (p. 90)

References

Graham, A. C. 1981. *Chuang-tzu, The Seven Inner Chapters and Other Writings fromthe Book Chuang-tzu.* London: George Allen and Unwin.

Guo Qingfan. 1983. *Zhuangzi Jishi.* Taipei: Muduo Press.

Larre, Claude. 1994. *The Way of Heaven: Neijing Suwen Chapters 1 and 2.* London:Monkey Press.

Wieger, L. 1965. *Chinese Characters: Their Origin, Etymology, History, Classification,and Signification: A Thorough Study from Chinese Documents.* Mincola, N.Y.: Dover Publications.

Wu, John C. H. 2006. *Lao Tzu. Tao Teh Ching.* Boston: Shambhala

www.ingramcontent.com/pod-product-compliance
Lightning Source LLC
Chambersburg PA
CBHW070550050426
42450CB00011B/2794